SPORTS MANIA!

Compete for the Gold in the sports trivia olympics. Every game you can think of is here, from baseball to skateboarding, from boxing to ice hockey. If you know your sports, you'll be a contender for the heavyweight trivia crown! Begin your warm up exercises with these sample stumpers:

— In what Ohio city did the Soap Box Derby originate?
— In 1965, Sonny Werblin made history by signing what player for $400,000?
— What sports tradition was originated by President William Howard Taft?
— Name baseball's three Alou brothers.
— Name the only player to steal seven bases in a seven game World Series.
— What two-step dance is named after a famous race horse?
— What famous actor was once a public address announcer at Ebbets Field?
— Who was "Gentlemen Jim?"
— When is an eagle not an eagle?
— What basketball team was originally known as the "Savoy Big Five?"

For answers to these and more than 1,000 other fascinating questions, keep on reading and surrender yourself to . . . **TRIVIA MANIA!**

SPORTS

TRIVIA Mania

XAVIER EINSTEIN

ZEBRA BOOKS
KENSINGTON PUBLISHING CORP.

The author would like to thank Jim and Judy Clark for their help in researching this book.

ZEBRA BOOKS

are published by

Kensington Publishing Corp.
475 Park Avenue South
New York, N.Y. 10016

First printing: June, 1984

Printed in the United States of America

TRIVIA MANIA: *Sports*

1) What is the original site of Madison Square Garden?

2) What was the first event staged at the new Madison Square Garden?

3) The movie "Bang the Drum Slowly" revolves around what major sport?

4) What trophy is awarded to the outstanding interior lineman in college football?

5) Rabbit Run is a novel dealing with what major sport?

6) What did Levy Burlingame do at the age of 80?

7) What sporting event begins with a "Tip-Off"?

8) Who was Dwight Eisenhower trying to tackle when he broke his leg?

. . . *Answers*

1. Madison & Fourth (there have actually been four sites in all)

2. Boxing

3. Baseball

4. The Outland Trophy

5. Basketball

6. Retired as an active jockey.

7. Basketball

8. Jim Thorpe

9) What was the nickname of Babe Ruth's bat?

10) Green Bay's star running back Paul Hornung played what position in college?

11) Which game ball is heaviest?
    a. golf
    b. paddle tennis
    c. court handball
    d. jai alai

12) A player's turn at a pool table is called . . .?
    a. a rack
    b. an inning
    c. a series
    d. a volley

13) What game was Alice in Wonderland playing using a flamingo and a hedgehog?
    a. golf
    b. bat and ball
    c. cricket
    d. croquet

14) Which of these games requires the use of english by the player?
    a. pool
    b. polo
    c. darts
    d. rugby

. . . Answers

9. "Black Betsy"

10. Quarterback

11. d.

12. b.

13. d.

14. a.

15) What is the distance between bases on a softball field?

16) What do the following names have in common? Kay Bell, Goldie Sellers, Blanch Martin and Laurie Walquist.

17) In what sport is the team judged on Canopy Display events?

18) In what sport do the participants go "bowl riding"?

19) In what sport is the participant judged for "Tube Rides"?

20) A Lutz, Camel and a Salchow are performed in what type event?

21) What has the fastest initial velocity, an arrow or a golf ball?

22) What did Roberta Gibb Bingay do in 1966?

23) Who was voted "Woman Athlete of the Half Century" in 1950?

The following quotes are credited to well known sports figures. Can you tell who?

24) "The bigger they come, the harder they fall."

25) "Win one for the Gipper."

. . . Answers

15. 60$'$

16. They are all men and play or played Pro Football.

17. Parachuting

18. Skateboard

19. Surfing

20. Figure skating

21. Golf ball — 170 MPH

22. Broke the sex barrier in the Boston Marathon.

23. Babe Dedrikson

24. Heavyweight Bob Fitzsimmons

25. Notre Dame's Knute Rockne

QUESTIONS

The following quotes are credited to well known sports figures. Can you tell who?

26) "Winning isn't everything, it's the only thing."

27) "Nice guys finish last."

28) "He can run, but he can't hide."

29) "It's not over until it's over."

30) In the movie "The Hustler" Paul Newman earned his living at what game?

31) What were Dizzy and Daffy Dean's real first names?

32) Who was the first black player elected to the Pro Football Hall of Fame?

33) Who pitched for the Chicago White Sox and also played forward for the Detroit Pistons?

34) Name the American baseball player who has more career homeruns than Hank Aaron?

35) Who formed and coached the Harlem Globetrotters?

36) Who held the heavyweight boxing title the longest?

. . . Answers

26. Green Bay's Vince Lombardi

27. Baseball's Leo Durocher

28. Heavyweight Champ Joe Louis

29. Who else? Yogi Berra

30. Pool or Pocket Billiards

31. Jerome (Jay Hanna) & Paul, respectively

32. Emlen Tunnell

33. Dave Debusschere

34. Josh Gibson of the Negro League

35. Abe Saperstein

36. Joe Louis had the longest reign of a heavyweight boxing champion: 11 years, 8 months, 7 days.

Who played the movie role of these famous sports figures?

37) Lou Gehrig

38) Brian Piccolo

39) Elroy Hirsch

40) Babe Ruth

41) Grover Cleveland Alexander

42) Monte Stratton

43) Knute Rockne

44) Gale Sayers

45) What college football player scored the first five times he had the ball in his first game?

46) What was the first horse to win over $2 million in purses?

47) In 1944 the Sullivan Award was won by a woman for the first time, name her.

48) In her career she won the Nat'l AAU Championships in five events (80 meter hurdles, high jump, shotput, javelin and baseball throw). Name her.

. . . Answers

37. Gary Cooper

38. James Caan

39. Elroy Hirsch

40. William Bendix

41. Ronald Reagan

42. Jimmy Stewart

43. Pat O'Brien

44. Billy D. Williams

45. Red Grange

46. Affirmed

47. Ann Curtis — swimmer

48. Babe Dedrikson

49) How many players to an Ultimate Frizbee team?

50) What was "The Miracle of Coogan's Bluff"?

51) What is the "Grapefruit League"?

52) Who were the "Whiz Kids"?

53) What was Johnny Vander Meer's never duplicated feat?

54) When two games are played in the same arena on the same day/evening, this is called?

55) Which defensive position does "the designated hitter" usually play during a game?

56) What sports tradition was originated by President William Howard Taft?

57) Who was the Minnesota Vikings first head coach?

58) What is the "pole sitter"?

59) In what year did the modern Olympics play their first summer games?

60) Walker Smith was the real name of what professional fighter? Hint: He held both the middleweight & welterweight crowns.

61) Who are the Broadway Blues?

. . . Answers

49. Seven

50. Bobby Thompson's famous 1951 playoff home-run.

51. Baseball's spring training

52. The 1950 Philadelphia Phillies

53. Pitched back-to-back no-hitters.

54. Double header or twin bill.

55. None

56. Throwing out the first ball of the season.

57. Norm Van Brocklin.

58. The car with the fastest qualifying time.

59. 1896

60. Sugar Ray Robinson

61. N.Y. Rangers

62) How did Jimmy Carter protest the Soviet invasion of Afghanistan?

63) Who replaced Weeb Ewbank as head coach of the Baltimore Colts?

64) In 1965 Sonny Werblin made history by signing what player for $400,000?

65) During the 1925 season, Yankee first baseman Wally Pipp sat out a game. What did his replacement do?

66) What is the diameter of a golf hole?

67) What horse won the thoroughbred's Triple Crown in 1973?

68) How many "spots" are there across the lane of a bowling alley?

69) In what sport do they run the Can-Am?

70) What leading money winning thoroughbred horse was named after a female tennis champion?

71) Who was the last NHL goalie to not wear a face mask?

72) British sprinter, Harold Abrahms of the 1924 Paris Olympics (Chariots of Fire) was proficient at what other track event?

. . . Answers

62. Boycotted the 1980 Summer Olympics.

63. Don Shula

64. Joe Namath

65. Play the next 2,130 consecutive games. It was Lou Gehrig.

66. 4¼ inches

67. Secretariat

68. Seven

69. Auto racing

70. Evert

71. Gump Worsley

72. Long jumper

QUESTIONS

73) Who KO'd Jersey Joe Walcott to win the World Heavyweight Championship, which he then never relinquished?

74) In 1965, the Chicago Bears had a rookie sensation who scored 22 touchdowns. Who was he?

Where did these famous basketball stars play their collegiate ball? Match the stars to their schools.

Player	College
75) Pete Maravich	a. Southern Illinois
76) Oscar Robertson	b. Princeton
77) Kareem Abduhl-Jabbar	c. LSU
78) Jerry Lucas	d. UCLA
79) Walt Frazier	e. Kansas
80) Spencer Haywood	f. DePaul
81) Elgin Baylor	g. Jacksonville
82) Artis Gilmore	h. Cincinnati
83) George Mikan	i. Ohio State
84) Bill Bradley	j. Detroit
85) Wilt Chamberlain	k. Seattle

. . . Answers

73. Rocky Marciano

74. Gale Sayers

75. c.

76. h.

77. d.

78. i.

79. a.

80. j.

81. k.

82. g.

83. f.

84. b.

85. e.

QUESTIONS

86) Name baseball's three Alou brothers.

87) Name the most recent set of twins to play major league baseball.

88) In 1951 Sugar Ray Robinson regained his middleweight title from what English fighter?

89) What sports shrine is located in Canton, Ohio?

90) Who won the Masters Golf Championship three times during the 1960's?

91) Name the ex-Dodger manager whose playing career lasted for only one at bat.

92) Who is the only American League player to hit at least three home runs in a game, twice in one year?

93) Spencer Haywood played for what ABA team?

94) What does the green lamp indicate at the goal judge's cage?

95) Name the Dodger pitcher who played his entire 14 year career under one manager.

96) What was the site of the first modern Olympic games?

97) Who did Jersey Joe Walcott win the heavyweight title from on July 18, 1951?

. . . _Answers_

86. Jesus, Matty & Felipe

87. Eddie & Johnny O'Brien

88. Randy Turpin

89. Pro Football Hall of Fame

90. Jack Nicklaus

91. Walter Alston

92. Ted Williams

93. Denver Rockets

94. End of period or game

95. Don Drysdale

96. Athens, Greece

97. Ezzard Charles

98) In racing terms, what are "slicks"?

99) What game begins with a "face-off"?

100) Name the three major league players to have over 6000 total bases.

101) What was the first racing commission to license a female jockey?

102) Who is the only American diver to win two gold medals in consecutive Olympics?

103) Who holds the National League record for consecutive games played by an outfielder?

104) What pitcher holds the record for most games won for a left hander?

105) In 1975, he broke John Unitas' career records for: most TD passes, most completions and most pass attempts.

106) What term is used to describe the fastest-accelerating dragster?

107) How many years did Wilt Chamberlain win the NCAA MVP award?

108) What is Amerathon '84?

109) When both teams in a hockey game are at full strength, how many players are on the ice?

. . . Answers

98. Smooth racing tires — no tread.

99. Hockey

100. Stan Musial, Willie Mays & Hank Aaron

101. Maryland

102. Pat McCormick 1952 — 1956

103. 1117 by Billy Williams

104. Warren Spahn

105. Fran Tarkenton

106. Top Fuel Eliminator

107. Once, 1957

108. Scheduled 39,000 mile road rally. Longest ever.

109. Twelve

110) The Baby Ruth candy bar was named after Babe Ruth. True or False?

111) The Green Monster is in San Francisco. True or False?

112) The NY Mets have never won a World Series. True or False?

113) Lou Gehrig holds the all time record for consecutive games played. True or False?

114) The book "Joy in Mudville" was about the NY Mets. True or False?

115) Only one man has pitched in the major leagues for 22 consecutive years. True or False?

116) Hank Aaron hit his 715th homerun in a game against the Montreal Expos. True or False?

117) Joe DiMaggio had his 56 game hitting streak in 1941. True or False?

118) Reggie Jackson and Babe Ruth are the only players to hit 3 homeruns in one game of a world series. True or False?

119) In the 1951 National League playoffs, Bobby Thompson hit his famous "Shot Heard Around the World" off Dodger pitcher Don Newcombe. True or False?

. . . Answers

110. False

111. False (It's in Fenway Park, Boston.)

112. False (They did it once in 1969.)

113. True (2,130)

114. True (It's not "Casey at the Bat.")

115. False

116. False (L.A. Dodgers)

117. True

118. True

119. False (Ralph Branca)

120) Billy Martin used to play third base for the NY Yankees. True or False?

121) Tom Seaver holds the record for consecutive strike outs in one game. True or False?

122) Babe Ruth is the only major league pitcher to ever hit a grand-slam. True or False?

123) When the American League was originally formed in 1901, Baltimore was one of the franchise cities. True or False?

124) On a fielder's choice, the batter is not credited for either a base hit or an at bat. True or False?

125) The Atlanta Braves are in the Western Division of the National League. True or False?

126) What sports distinction does Kathy Kusner hold?

127) Which of the following is illegal in an ice hockey game? A hand pass or a skate pass.

128) In the '69–'70 season, he won the following titles in the ABA: MVP, rookie of the year, MVP All-Star Game, scoring average leader, rebounding leader.

129) What phrase signals the start of the INDY 500?

130) How many dimples on a golf ball?

. . . Answers

120. False (2nd base)

121. True

122. False (It's been done a number of times.)

123. True (They were called the Orioles then too.)

124. False Batter is charged with an at-bat.)

125. True (Seems odd, but it is true.)

126. First U.S. women granted a jockey's license.

127. Hand pass

128. Spencer Haywood

129. "Gentlemen, start your engines."

130. 336

QUESTIONS

131) Name the only player to steal 7 bases in a 7 game World Series.

132) What was the first year the USSR sent a team to the summer Olympics?

133) Who dominated the NBA in average assists for 8 consecutive years between 1952 and 1960?

134) In 1977 the Atlanta Falcons set an NFL record for fewest points given up in a season. How many?

135) Who was the first player born outside continental US elected to baseball's Hall of Fame?

136) Mary, Queen of Scots and her cousin Elizabeth I were skilled players at what game?

137) What player holds the major league record for being hit by a pitch most times in one year?

138) First American woman to swim the English channel from France to England.

139) What is "Whitey" Ford's full name?

140) What is the height and width of a hockey goal?

141) How many years did Connie Mack manage the Philadelphia Athletics?

142) How many players per side in Canadian football?

. . . *Answers*

131. Lou Brock

132. 1952

133. Bob Cousy

134. 129

135. Roberto Clemente

136. Billiards

137. Ron Hunt

138. Gertrude Ederle

139. Edward Charles Ford

140. Six feet wide, four feet high

141. Fifty years

142. Twelve

143) What two-step dance is named after a famous race horse?

144) What famous sporting event was last held in the 392 A.D.?

145) In 1922 Ty Cobb bats .401 but loses the batting crown to who?

146) The last time this occurred at the INDY 500 was in 1931. What was it?

147) Who was the lightest heavyweight to fight a championship fight?

148) Willie Mays' memorable over the shoulder catch at the Polo grounds came off whose bat?

149) Buddy Young played for what All-American Conference football team during the 40's?

150) What female sprinter won the Sullivan award as amateur athlete of the year 1961.

. . . *Answers*

143. Dan Patch

144. The ancient Olympic games

145. George Sisler, .420

146. The winner averaged less than 100 MPH (96.629)

147. Bob Fitzsimmons, 167 lbs.

148. Vic Wertz

149. New York Yankees

150. Wilma Rudolf

QUESTIONS

Race drivers receive instructions during a race by officials signalling with flags. How well can you match the flags and signals listed below?

Flag	Signal
151) Black	a. Course is slippery
152) Red	b. Non-racing car on course
153) Yellow	c. Driver must stop
154) Checkered	d. Another car is following
155) Blue	f. All drivers must stop
156) Yellow with red stripes	f. Caution, do not pass
157) White	g. End of race

158) In 1952 she became the first American skier to win two Olympic gold medals.

159) What did Bob Nieman do his first two times at bat as a major league player in 1951?

160) Name the only brothers to each hit a home run in an All-Star game.

161) Where was the famous sign: "Hit the sign, win a suit"?

162) If a pool player is given "Cue ball in hand," what may the player do with it?

163) Heavyweight Champion Floyd Patterson won an Olympic gold medal in what weight class?

. . . Answers

151. c.

152. e.

153. f.

154. g.

155. d.

156. a.

157. b.

158. Andrea Mead Lawrence

159. Hit home runs

160. Vince & Joe DiMaggio

161. Ebbets Field

162. Place it anywhere on the table

163. Middleweight

164) Jackie Robinson was a scoring champion at UCLA in what sport?

165) Pro golfer Gary Player hails from what country?

166) Where did the Dallas Cowboys play before moving to Texas Stadium?

167) Name the only two brothers to pitch against each other in a National League game.

168) In auto racing; a single seat, open-cockpit, tubular body and engine located behind driver describes what kind of vehicle?

169) Name the US city which has twice hosted the winter Olympic games?

170) What was so unusual about St. Louis Browns' outfielder Pete Gray?

171) Around the NHL he was known as "the rocket".

172) Who was the first Washington Redskin to ever gain over 1,000 yards rushing in a season?

173) In what sport is it illegal to palm, travel or goaltend?

174) Who set an all-time record for women's golf, winning 17 consecutive tournaments?

. . . Answers

164. Basketball

165. South Africa

166. Cotton Bowl

167. Phil & Joe Niekro

168. Formula Car

169. Lake Placid, 1932 & 1980

170. He only had one arm

171. Maurice Richard

172. Larry Brown, 1970

173. Basketball

174. Babe Dedrikson

175) Who won the men's "Pro Bowler of the Year" four times during the decade of the 50's?

Name the teams christened with these defensive nicknames.

176) "Doomsday Defense"

177) "No-name Defense"

178) "Orange Crush"

179) "Silver Rush"

180) Fearsome Foursome

181) What was Jessie Owens nickname?

182) Approximately 90% of all thoroughbred horses are descended from what 18th century Arabian stallion?

183) What famous actor was once a public address announcer at Ebbets Field?

184) What is the professional name of Robert Craig Knievel?

185) How many players on a polo team?

186) Harry Stuhldreher, Don Miller, Jim Crowley and Elmer Layden were better known as . . . ?

. . . Answers

175. Don Carter

176. Dallas Cowboys

177. Miami Dolphins

178. Denver Broncos

179. Detroit Lions

180. L.A. Rams

181. Ebony Express

182. Eclipse

183. John Forsythe

184. Evil Knievel

185. Four

186. The Four Horseman of Notre Dame

187) When "Mighty Casey" struck out to end the game, what was the final score?

188) At what age does a filly become a mare?

189) How many teeth does a horse have—male or female?

190) If a 15 round bout goes "the distance," what is the total elapsed time from the opening bell?

191) They lived across the street from each other, their fathers worked for the same company and they both became major league catchers. Who are they?

192) What is the name of the Air Force Academy's football team?

193) What three weapons are used in fencing?

194) Name two members of the baseball Hall of Fame who were never in organized ball?

195) What was it called before becoming the "Americas Cup"?

196) Name the famous brothers who were both heavyweight fighters and had film careers?

197) Who was the first person to break the 4 minute mile?

. . . Answers

187. 4 to 2 (the score stood 2 to 4. . .)

188. 5 years

189. 40-male, 36-female

190. 59 minutes

191. Yogi Berra & Joe Garagiola

192. The Falcons

193. Foil, epee and saber

194. Bud Abbott and Lou Costello, "Who's on First"

195. Queens Cup

196. Max & Buddy Baer

197. Roger Bannister

198) Who did Bowie Kuhn replace as Baseball Commissioner in 1969?

199) What are 6 ways a batter can get on base without getting a hit?

200) "Big Six" was the nickname given to what pitching great?

201) Which golf tournament is played over these three courses? Pebble Beach, Spy Glass Hill, Cypress Point.

202) What major league team was implicated in the 1919 World Series "Black Sox Scandal"?

203) The Borg-Warner Trophy is given to whom?

204) What do Cotton, Orange, Peach, Rose, Sugar and Tangerine all have in common?

205) In the movie "Pride of the Yankees" who played Babe Ruth?

206) Who was "Gentleman Jim"?

207) What comprises the Grand Slam of Tennis?

. . . Answers

198. General William Eckart

199. Error, hit by pitch, dropped 3rd strike, interference, fielder's choice.

200. Christy Mathewson

201. Bing Crosby Open

202. Chicago White Sox

203. Winner of Indy 500

204. College Football Bowls

205. Babe Ruth

206. Prizefighter James J. Corbett

207. French, U.S., Australian Opens, and Wimbledon

QUESTIONS

Can you pick the team match-ups for each Super Bowl and also name the winner? Note: Some match-ups have met for more than one Super Bowl.

Super Bowl	Teams
208) I, 1967	a. New York and Baltimore
209) II, 1968	b. Miami and Dallas
210) III, 1969	c. Pittsburgh and Minnesota
211) IV, 1970	d. Cincinnati and San Francisco
212) V, 1971	e. Oakland and Minnesota
213) VI, 1972	f. Kansas City and Green Bay
214) VII, 1973	g. Oakland and Philadelphia
215) VIII, 1974	h. Baltimore and Dallas
216) IX, 1975	i. Miami and Washington
217) X, 1976	j. Pittsburgh and Dallas
218) XI, 1977	k. Oakland and Green Bay
219) XII, 1978	l. Los Angeles Raiders and Washington
220) XIII, 1979	
221) XIV, 1980	m. Pittsburgh and Los Angeles
222) XV, 1981	n. Kansas City and Minnesota
223) XVI, 1982	o. Denver and Dallas
224) XVII, 1983	p. Miami and Minnesota
225) XVIII, 1984	

226) Who was the first president of the NFL?

227) What was the first tournament Jack Nicklaus won after joining the PGA tour?

228) In what sport do you find "barrel racing"?

229) What did Nina Kusnik accomplish in 1972?

43

. . . Answers

208. f — Green Bay
209. k — Green Bay
210. a — New York
211. n — Kansas City
212. h — Baltimore
213. b — Dallas
214. i — Miami
215. p — Miami
216. c — Pittsburgh
217. m — Pittsburgh
218. e — Oakland
219. o — Dallas
220. j — Pittsburgh
221. m — Pittsburgh
222. g — Oakland
223. d — San Francisco
224. i — Washington
225. l — Los Angeles Raiders
226. Jim Thorpe
227. U.S. Open
228. Rodeo
229. First woman to officially complete the Boston Marathon

230) Forced out of pro-tennis by a heart attack, he became Captain-coach of the U.S. Davis team.

231) The play and film "The Great White Hope" was based on whose life?

232) They call him "The Big O". Who is he?

233) He held the record for fewest strike outs in a season for 12 consecutive seasons.

234) Who eclipsed Don Maynard's record of most receptions lifetime?

235) Who did Primo Carnera KO to win the heavyweight title?

236) When is an eagle not an eagle?

237) He was the NCAA MVP three years in a row, '67, '68 & '69.

238) Czonka, Warfield & Kick left the Miami Dolphins to play for what team?

239) If a saddle bronc rider "pulls leather", what is he doing?

240) What are the Alpine events in skiing?

. . . *Answers*

230. Arthur Ashe

231. Jack Johnson — The world's first black heavy-weight champion

232. Oscar Robertson

233. Nellie Fox

234. Charley Taylor

235. Jack Sharkey

236. When it's a hole-in-one. (Par 3 hole)

237. Lew Alcindor

238. Memphis of the World Football League

239. Holding onto the saddle

240. Downhill, Slalom & Giant Slalom

241) He has the most Daytona 500 wins.
   a. Richard Petty
   b. A.J. Foyt
   c. Cale Yarlborough
   d. Bobby Allison

242) He won the INDY 500 three times between 1971–1980.
   a. A.J. Foyt
   b. Bobby Unser
   c. Johnny Rutherford
   d. Gordon Johncock

243) In the first sponsored U.S. auto race, run between Chicago and Evanston, Illinois, the average speed was?
   a. 7.5 MPH
   b. 17.5 MPH
   c. 47.5 MPH
   d. 67.5 MPH

244) Nitromethane is used for what purpose?
   a. Medicate long distance runners for exhaustion
   b. High performance racing fuel
   c. Drug detection in athletes
   d. None of the above

245) The winner of the American College Unions Championship is:
   a. an archer
   b. billiards player
   c. a gymnast
   d. a bronco rider

. . . Answers

241. a. Richard Petty

242. c. Johnny Rutherford

243. a. 7.5 MPH

244. b. High performance racing fuel

245. b. a billiards player

246) Name the only brothers in major league history to win a league batting championship.

247) A pool player trying to distract his opponent may be called for what violation?

248) Which Olympic games were cancelled as a result of World War I?

249) The NIT is always played at what site?

250) Who had the record for most career home runs by a switch hitter?

251) What is significant about the 1958 Daytona auto race?

252) The book "Man Against Himself" is about what sport?

253) In 1972 Larry Czonka and Mercury Morris both accomplished the same feat for the Miami Dolphins. What was it?

254) Before losing to the Russians in 1972, the U.S. basketball team had compiled how many consecutive victories?

255) Name the three American League teams that do not play for a specific city.

. . . Answers

246. Harry Walker — 1947
     Dixie Walker — 1944

247. Sharking

248. 1916 summer Olympics

249. Madison Square Garden

250. Mickey Mantle

251. Last time it was run on the beach.

252. Auto racing

253. Ran for 1000 yards each

254. 62

255. California Angels, Texas Rangers, Minnesota Twins

256) Who is the only person to win the Wimbledon singles title eight times?

257) Where is the Baseball Hall of Fame located?

258) Where is the Basketball Hall of Fame?

259) What year were batting helmets introduced to the major league?

260) What is Joe Namath's nickname?

261) What does Wilt Chamberlain always wear on his right wrist?

262) Who was the "Galloping Ghost?"

263) Who was the "Georgia Peach"?

264) Who was the only player to hit a fair ball out of Yankee Stadium (exhibition game)?

265) Who was "the barber"?

266) What college football game might be preceded by an appearance by "The Golden Knights" precision parachuting team?

267) In what sports do you find a brassie, a spoon, and a baffy/cleek?

268) Who was the "Grand Old Man" of football?

... *Answers*

256. Helen Wills Moody, 1927, 28, 29, 30, 32, 33, 35 & 38.

257. Cooperstown, N.Y.

258. Springfield College, Springfield, MA.

259. 1941

260. "Broadway Joe"

261. A rubber band

262. Harold "Red" Grange

263. Ty Cobb

264. Josh Gibson

265. Pitcher Sal Maglie

266. Army

267. Golf

268. Amos Alonzo Stagg

QUESTIONS

269) What basketball team was originally known as the "Savoy Big Five"?

270) No one has ever hit a fair ball out of Yankee Stadium in a major league game. True or False?

271) N.Y. Knicks great Bill Bradley was also a Rhodes Scholar. True or False?

272) The Olympics have always been limited to amateur sports competition. True or False?

273) Joe Walcott was the World Welterweight Champion from 1898–1906. True or False?

274) One of Fran Tarkenton's many passing records is most interceptions. True or False?

275) It is safe to stand in a fairway holding a one-iron over your head during a thunderstorm. True or False?

276) Down hill skiers have been clocked at over 120 MPH. True or False?

277) Reading poetry was an event during the 1914 and 1922 Olympics. True or False?

278) Actually there are really 11 teams in college football's Big Ten Conference. True or False?

279) The real last name of the Alou brothers is Rojas. True or False?

. . . Answers

269. Harlem Globe Trotters

270. True

271. True

272. False

273. True (It's not Jersey Joe)

274. False

275. True (Every golfer knows that even God can't hit a one iron.)

276. True

277. False (neither was an Olympic year)

278. False

279. True

280) No one ever pitched a no-hitter in Forbes Field, Pittsburgh Stadium from 1909–1970. True or False?

281) In golf, the longer shot would normally be hit with a 1 wood or a 4 wood.

282) They called him "Lefty" Grove. What was his full name?

283) What famous N.Y. Knicks star went on to become a U.S. Senator?

284) Who was on deck when Bobby Thompson hit his famous playoff home run?

285) Who was the U.S. Women's Figure Skating Champion in 1973–74?

286) This Olympic swimmer won the Sullivan Award as Amateur Athlete of the year. Who was it?

287) Who was the first player in the NHL to score 50 goals in a season?

288) In the year Roger Maris hit 61 home runs, how many times was he walked intentionally?

289) "Rosey" played offensive tackle for the N.Y. Giants from 1953–1965. What is his full name?

290) Rocco Barbella was a middleweight champ and is know by what name?

. . . *Answers*

280. True

281. 1 wood — Driver

282. Robert Moses Grove

283. Bill Bradley

284. Willie Mays

285. Dorothy Hamill

286. Mark Spitz

287. Maurice Richard

288. None (Mantle was on deck)

289. Roosevelt Brown

290. Rocky Graziano

291) Is left field to the pitcher's left or the batters left?

292) Who holds the NBA record for most free throws made in a single season?

293) When Joe DiMaggio hit in 56 consecutive games, whose record did he eclipse and what was that record?

294) What distinction is associated with the 1914 Middleweight title fight between A. McCoy & G. Chip?

295) This platform diver won an unprecedented 3 consecutive gold medals in platform diving competition in 1968, 1972 & 1976 — he also earned a silver in 1964, name him.

296) Who works from the "Rubber"?

297) Who holds the NBA record for most career assists?

298) What NFL team was featured in the movie, "Number One"?

299) What Olympic Fighter, banned from the medal awards, went on to become World Heavyweight Champion?

300) Gertrude Ederle won an Olympic Gold Medal in which event?

. . . Answers

291. Batter's left

292. Jerry West, 1965-66

293. Wee Willie Keeler, 44 games

294. Shortest title fight ever — 45 seconds

295. Klaus Dibiasi

296. The pitcher

297. Oscar Robertson

298. New Orleans Saints

299. Ingemar Johanson

300. 400 meter relay

301) She left the streets of Harlem a virtual unknown & returned from England in 1951 with the Wimbledon Title. Name her.

302) In 1916 Mordecai "Three Fingers" Brown and what other famous pitcher pitched their final career games on the same day and against each other?

303) The first football game ever was played between which 2 teams?

304) How high is the basketball hoop from the floor?

305) The first AL-NL All-Star Game was played what year?

306) Dempsey vs. Carpentier, July 2, 1921, has what distinction?

307) Who was the only man to be both rookie of the year and manager of the year?

308) Who won the first computerized "All-Time Heavyweight Championship"?

309) When was the last major league game played in Boston's Braves Field?

310) Billie Jean King shares the record of 19 combined Wimbledon Titles with what other American tennis great?

. . . *Answers*

301. Althea Gibson

302. Christy Mathewson

303. Rutgers & Princeton

304. 10 feet

305. 1933

306. First radio broadcast of a prizefight.

307. Bill Virdon

308. Rocky Marciano

309. Sept. 21, 1952

310. Elizabeth Ryan

311) What was the last year Jackie Robinson played for the Dodgers?

312) What group originated the NIT?

313) What American sister-brother team won the Wimbledon mixed doubles championship in 1980?

314) Who was the midget who played for the St. Louis Browns?

Name the university the following Pro Football players attended:

315) Steve Bartkowski   A. Iowa

316) Jim Brown   B. California

317) John Hadl   C. Notre Dame

318) Alex Karras   D. Illinois

319) Johnny Lujack   E. Kansas

320) Roger Staubach   F. Tulsa

321) Howard Twilley   G. Navy

322) Buddy Young   H. Syracuse

323) Primo Carnera lost his heavyweight title to . . . ?

. . . *Answers*

311. 1956

312. The NY City Basketball Writers

313. Tracy & John Austin

314. Eddie Gaedel — 43 in.

315. B.

316. H.

317. E.

318. A.

319. C.

320. G.

321. F.

322. D.

323. Max Baer

324) What NHL hockey team once boasted a father & his two sons on the same team?

325) Who now governs the NIT?

326) Joe Louis was heavyweight champion between what years?

327) In what year did the modern Olympics play their first winter games?

328) Where is the Women's Professional Billiard Alliance Hall of Fame located?

329) Name the only major league player to die as a result of an injury incurred during a game?

330) Name the last league baseball team to break the color barrier?

331) What NBA player was the field goal percentage leader in 6 out of 10 years between 1960 & 1970?

332) Who is the only Braves player to play in all 3 franchise cities, Boston, Milwaukee & Atlanta?

333) What years were the summer Olympics cancelled as a result of WW II.

334) In what sport will you find "short rack games"?

. . . Answers

324. Whalers (Hartford)

325. Eastern Collegiate Athletic Conference

326. 1937-1949

327. 1924

328. Brooklyn, N.Y.

329. Ray Chapman

330. Boston Red Sox

331. Wilt Chamberlain

332. Eddie Mathews

333. 1940 & 1944

334. Billiards

335) Name the only major league player to get 3 hits in one inning.

336) Is a blocked punt a "live" ball or a "dead" ball?

337) Wilt Chamberlain has scored over 100 points in one game, against what team?

338) How many times did Muhammed Ali win the heavyweight crown?

339) Name the first black player in the American League.

340) Grenoble was the site of the 10th winter Olympic games in 1968. What country is that in?

341) What football team boasted the famous combination of Blanchard to Davis?

342) Who completed a string of 294 consecutive passes without an interception between 1964 & 1965?

343) Who was the first American to win the men's singles championship at Wimbledon?

344) Where did Cazzie Russel play his college ball?

345) Who was the only baseball player to have the same last name as the town he was born in?

. . . Answers

335. Gene Stephens

336. Live ball

337. N.Y. Knicks

338. 3

339. Larry Doby

340. France

341. Army Football

342. Bart Starr (Green Bay)

343. Bill Tilden

344. Michigan

345. Estel Crabtree from Crabtree, Ohio

346) The ball the cue ball strikes (not in combination) is called what?

347) Name the only father & son pitchers in major league history to both lead the league in losses one year.

348) What was the original name of the N.Y. Jets?

349) Who held the light-heavyweight crown for 10 years?

350) What was the point of controversy in the Russian win over the U.S. basketball team during the 1972 Olympics?
   a. Sneakers
   b. The clock
   c. Drugs
   d. Spectator interference

351) What was unique about the James J. Corbett - Bob Fitzsimmons fight on March 17, 1897?
   a. First time gloves were worn
   b. It was fought under lights
   c. First fight ever filmed
   d. Boxer trunks replaced normal leotards

352) In Ebbets Field he hit the "Hit this sign, win a suit" twice. Only three others hit it once. Who was he?
   a. Duke Snider
   b. Carl Furillo
   c. Jackie Robinson
   d. Gil Hodges

. . . Answers

346. The object ball

347. Duane & Herman Pillette

348. N.Y. Titans

349. Archie Moore

350. b. The clock

351. c. First fight ever filmed

352. b. Carl Furillo

353) The 1937 Triple Crown was won by . . . ?
   a. War Admiral
   b. Secretariat
   c. Man O'War
   d. Dark Mirage

354) In what sport do the participants compete in the Grand Nationals?
   a. Auto racing
   b. Equestrian
   c. Trotters
   d. Golf

355) Lou Gehrig was nicknamed "The Iron Horse." What did his teammates call him?
   a. Buster
   b. Lou-Lou
   c. Gerry
   d. Babe Jr.

356) Who was the oldest rookie in the NBA at age 29. Hint: He played for the Phoenix Suns.
   a. Joe Palchick
   b. Nat Holman
   c. Connie Hawkins
   d. Bob Cousy

357) Who was the first black player to win the Heisman Trophy.
   a. Dick "Night Train" Lane   c. Emlen Tunnell
   b. Jim Brown   d. Ernie Davis

. . . *Answers*

353. a. War Admiral

354. a. Auto racing

355. a. Buster

356. c. Connie Hawkins

357. d. Ernie Davis

358) What is the maximum allowable number of clubs in a golfer's bag?
   a. 11
   b. 12
   c. 13
   d. 14

359) She won the Billiard Congress of America U.S. Open every year from 1972–1977.

360) Which original Mets' player played the longest for the Mets?

361) Bud Wilkinson earned his winning reputation coaching which college football team during the '50's?

362) Carmen Basilio held two different boxing titles, name them . . .

363) How many winter Olympic games were cancelled as a result of WW II?

364) What driver won the INDY 500 three times during the 1960's?

365) Name the only non-Yankee to hit more than 10 World Series home runs.

366) How many times did he win the NBA scoring championship as Lew Alcindor?

. . . *Answers*

358. d. 14

359. Jean Balukas

360. Ed Kranepool

361. Oklahoma Sooners

362. Welterweight & Middleweight

363. Two — 1940 and 1944

364. A.J. Foyt

365. Duke Snider

366. Once

367) Name the great Chicago Bears quarterback who threw seven TD passes against the Giants in 1943.

368) Who did Ezzard Charles decision in 15 rounds to win the heavyweight crown in 1949?

369) The US Olympic basketball winning streak of 62 games ended in 1972, what year did it begin?

370) What US man won the World Figure Skating Championship in 1948–49?

371) Who holds the record for most home runs by a catcher in a single season?

372) In 1930, the Chicago Bears signed a great rookie by the name of Bronco . . . ?

373) Wilt Chamberlain holds almost every individual scoring record, including one he would rather do without. What is it?

374) What was the shortest heavyweight title fight on record?

375) Who was the first Olympic swimmer to earn 4 gold medals in one Olympic?

376) Who hit the first pinch hit home run in an All-Star Game?

Answers

367. Sid Luckman

368. Joe Walcott

369. 1936

370. Dick Button

371. Johnny Bench

372. Nagurski

373. Most missed free throws in a game. He had 22.

374. Ali vs. Liston, Lewiston, Maine one minute

375. Don Schollander

376. Mickey Owen

377) Who said, "Don't look back, something may be gaining on you".

378) What was the irony about Al Downing pitching Hank Aarons' 715th home run?

379) Max Baer lost his heavyweight crown to . . . ?

380) Who holds the major league record for the most pinch-hit home runs in a season?

381) How many Olympic games were cancelled as a result of World War I?

382) How many times did Ray Robinson win the middleweight crown?

383) Who holds the major league record for most hits in one game?

384) The Denver Broncos play their home games in which stadium?

385) Kareem Abduhl-Jabbar used to play under what name?

386) Name the only pitcher to win 20 games in a season pitching in both leagues.

387) Who did Joe Louis win the heavyweight title from?

. . . Answers

377. Satchel Page

378. He wore the same number as Aaron, 44

379. James Braddock

380. Johnny Frederick

381. One

382. Five

383. John Burnett

384. Mile High Stadium

385. Lew Alcindor

386. Hank Borowi

387. James Braddock

388) If the Hoyas played the Terrapins on national TV, who are they & what are they playing?

389) Who caught the final out in the 1969 World Series?

390) In what way did Jimmy Pearsall celebrate hitting his 200th home run?

391) Who was the first woman to ever qualify for the INDY 500?

392) Who was baseball's first black manager?

393) What was the last year the AFL played an All-Star Game?

394) Floyd Patterson suffered a first round KO, on Sept. 25, 1962 at the hands of whom?

395) At what ball park was the first major league base-ball game televised in 1939?

396) In what game can a player be "picked-off"?

397) In what games do the players "spike" the ball.

398) What's a "mulligan"?

399) What is the "Grapefruit League"?

Answers

388. Georgetown vs Maryland, College Basketball

389. Cleon Jones

390. He ran backwards around the bases

391. Janet Guthrie

392. Frank Robinson

393. 1970

394. Sonny Liston

395. Ebbets Field

396. Baseball

397. Volleyball & Football

398. A "do over" in golf

399. Baseball's spring training

400) NASCAR champion Lee Petty did not become a professional race car driver until he was 35 years old. True or False?

401) Over 25 million tennis balls are used world wide each year. True or False?

402) Bruce Jenner's total point score of 8,618 was the largest ever in Olympic decathlon history. True or False?

403) Tournament tennis balls must be either white, yellow or green. True or False?

404) Up until 1965 Olympic Freestyle swimmers were required to make a hand-touch on turns. True or False?

405) The small piece of rope a rodeo rider carries in his mouth when calf-roping is called a "pigging string". True or False?

406) In ice hockey, the team "checking" means verifying a player change with the referee. True or False?

407) How many Olympic gold medals did Sonja Henie win for figure skating.

408) In what year was night baseball introduced into the majors?

409) What team had the nickname "The Gashouse Gang"?

. . . Answers

400. True

401. True

402. True

403. False (white, yellow or orange)

404. True

405. True

406. False (stopping the puck handler by using the body)

407. Three, 1928, 1932 and 1936.

408. 1935

409. St. Louis Cardinals

410) What device do drag racers use to brake their cars at the end of a run.

411) The LA Lakers got their name when they played for what city?

412) What fighter had the shortest reign as heavyweight champion?

413) What side of the plate did Mickey Mantle bat from?

414) How old was Sonja Henie when she entered her first Olympic competition?

415) How many strides will an average-height sprinter take in a 100 meter race?

416) What is the current record in the British Lawn Mower Grand Prix? (1981)

417) From what city do the Atlanta Braves originally hail?

418) What pro quarterback holds the record for being intercepted the most times?

419) Who was the WBA World Heavyweight Champion between 1979–80?

420) A "passed ball" is an error charged to which player?

. . . Answers

410. A parachute

411. Minneapolis, Minn.

412. John Tate, 163 days

413. Both sides

414. 11 years old

415. 50

416. 37 MPH

417. Boston

418. George Blanda

419. "Big" John Tate

420. The catcher

421) Name the jockey who retired in 1966 with 32,407 rides to his record.

422) The NHL record for "most points by a rookie" is held by who? Hint: It happened in the 1980–81 season.

423) How many times has a perfect game been pitched in World Series competition?

424) His name is Edson Arantes do Nascimento and he comes from Brazil. The world knows him by what other name?

425) What happened on Sept. 29, 1957, in New York?

426) For how many seasons did Gordie Howe score the most points for the season?

427) Raiders' owner Al Davis once held an important post in pro-football. What was it?

428) During the '50s Sandy Saddler fought another great featherweight in four memorable fights. Who was it?

429) How many stitches are there on the seam of a baseball?

430) Who was known as "The Perfesser"?

431) In what event would the participants perform a Vertical "S" or a Cuban eight?

. . . Answers

421. Johnny Longden

422. Peter Stasny, Quebec

423. Only once, by Don Larsen of the Yankees

424. Pelé

425. Last Giants baseball game at the Polo Grounds.

426. Six '51, '52, '53, '54, '57, '63.

427. Commissioner AFL

428. Willie Pep

429. 108 double stitches

430. Casey Stengel

431. Aerobatic flying

432) What is the length of a bowling alley?

433) What is considered the fastest of all court games?

434) Who holds the NHL record for most assists by a goalie?

435) What franchise moved to Baltimore and became the Orioles?

436) What is the world speed record for water skiing?

437) How long did it take for the world's slowest racing pigeon to cover a distance of 370 miles?

438) The current record for single handed trans-Atlantic yacht racing is just over 20 days. The first race in 1891 took how long?

439) Which city once hosted 3 major league baseball teams at the same time?

440) What was the prize awarded the winner of the discus throw in the ancient Olympics?

441) What are the dimensions of a standard competition ice rink?

442) The divers at Acapulco dive from rocks 118 feet high. How deep is the water?

. . . Answers

432. 60 feet

433. Jai Alai

434. Mike Palmateer, Wash. Caps. '80-81

435. St. Louis Browns

436. 128.16 MPH

437. 7 years, 2 months

438. 45 days

439. New York — Yankees, Giants & Dodgers

440. The discus — it was made of bronze

441. 60x30 meters or 196 ft. x 98 ft.

442. 12 feet

443) What kind of wood is most commonly used to make baseball bats?

444) What was the last year the 200 meter Tandem Bicycle event was run in the Olympics?

445) 1934 was the last season this pitch was legal. Name this well known outlawed pitch.

446) In what game do you score for ringers and leaners?

447) Who holds the record for most games played by a major league baseball player?

448) In what sport do only the "jammers" score points?

449) How many points is a safety worth in football?

450) Which American League baseball team is not from an American city?

Can you name the cities these NBA teams hail from?

451) Hawks

452) Bulls

453) Cavaliers

454) Suns

455) Jazz

. . . *Answers*

443. Ash

444. 1972.

445. The Spitball

446. Horseshoes

447. Hank Aaron, 3298

448. Roller Derby

449. 2 points.

450. Toronto Blue Jays

451. Atlanta

452. Chicago

453. Cleveland

454. Phoenix

455. Utah

Can you name the cities these NBA teams hail from?

456) Pacers

457) Rockets

458) Clippers

459) Trailblazers

460) Kings

461) How many periods in a hockey game?

462) In what game does a team earn points only when they are not in possession of the ball.

463) What is the Calgary Stampede?

464) In what Olympic competition do you find a "pommel horse"?

465) The Indian Packing Company provided the equipment and the team name for what pro team?

466) Who was Paul Newman's technical advisor in the 1961 movie "The Hustler"?

467) What St. Louis Cardinal player once hit four home runs in four consecutive times at bat?

. . . Answers

456. Indiana

457. Houston

458. San Diego

459. Portland

460. Kansas City

461. Three

462. Baseball

463. Canada's most famous rodeo

464. Gymnastics

465. Green Bay Packers

466. Minnesota Fats

467. Stan Musial

468) At one time New York hosted four teams whose names all rhymed. Name them.

469) In tennis, what does the term "love" indicate?

470) Who broke Lou Brock's season record for most stolen bases?

471) Name the first NBA player to score 20,000 points.

472) Ty Cobb'ss uniform number was never retired. Why?

473) How long must a hockey player remain in the penalty box when serving a minor penalty?

474) What are the 5 "standard" competition events in a rodeo?

475) Where is the Sugar Bowl played?

476) Only one major league player has ever made a base hit for 2 different teams in the same day. Name him.

477) In bowling, what is the number of the 2nd pin in the third row?

478) Who coached UCLA to their first NCAA basketball championship?

. . . Answers

468. Mets, Jets, Nets & Sets

469. The score is zero

470. Rickey Henderson—Oakland A's

471. Bob Pettit, St. Louis Hawks

472. There were no numbers on uniforms when he retired.

473. 2 minutes

474. Bareback riding, saddle bronc and bull riding plus calf roping and steer wrestling. Other events may also be included.

475. New Orleans

476. Joel Youngblood—the day he was traded from the Mets to the Expo's

477. Five pin

478. John Wooden

479) What major league team played a game where all the managerial decisions were made on a vote by 1,115 "grandstand managers"?

480) How long is a football field, including the end zones?

481) Where is Churchill Downs located?

482) Who was the last U.S. Bareknuckle Champion?

483) How many times have the N.Y. Yankees won the World Series?

484) Who scored the winning touchdown in Baltimores' championship win of the Giants in 1958?

485) What NHL goalie has won the Vezina Trophy the most times?

486) The world's fastest recorded refueling pit stop took 4 seconds. True or False?

487) The first lineman elected to the Football Hall of Fame was Bruno Sammertino. True or False?

488) Bob Mathias won the Olympic decathlon not once, but twice 1948 & 1952. The only American to perform this feat. True or False?

489) The highest 3 game series ever bowled was 886. True or False?

. . . Answers

479. St. Louis Browns — Aug. 24, 1951

480. 120 yards

481. Lexington, Kentucky

482. John L. Sullivan

483. 22 times

484. Alan "the horse" Ameche

485. Jacques Plante — 7 times

486. True (1976 INDY 500, Bobby Unser's crew)

487. False (Bruno is a wrestler)

488. False (Rafer Johnson in 1956 & 1960 also)

489. True (Allie Brandt, 1939 — 297, 289, 300)

490) The Golden Gloves was originated and sponsored in 1927 by the Chicago Tribune. True or False?

491) Florence McCulcheon shocked the bowling world by losing by only 3 pins to champ Jimmy Smith during a man vs. woman exhibition match. True or False?

492) Willie Mosconi holds the pocket billiard record with a high run of 526. His run was interrupted by a spectator distraction. True or False?

493) Ty Cobb's lifetime batting average of .367 is the second highest in baseball history. True or False?

494) The Pittsburgh Steelers have been to the Super Bowl 4 times and never lost. True or False?

495) The Minnesota Vikings have won only once in their 4 Super Bowl aistarances. True or False?

496) The Vardon Trophy is awarded in pro Hockey. True or False?

497) Mark Spitz won 7 gold medals in Olympic swimming. True or False?

498) Golfer Gary Player's favorite playing color is black. True or False?

499) The longest recorded prizefight lasted 110 rounds. True or False?

. . . Answers

490. False (New York Daily News)

491. False (actually she beat him)

492. False (He just got tired and quit)

493. False (highest)

494. True

495. False (never won)

496. False (golf)

497. False (he won 9, two in '68 and seven in '72)

498. True

499. True

500) Who scored ahead of Bobby Thompson when he hit his "Shot heard around the world" in 1951?

501) What do tennis stars Maureen Connally and Margaret Court Smith have in common?

502) Who was the first black golfer to qualify for the Masters?

503) Who was the youngest player in the major leagues?

504) Who was named the greatest basketball player for the first half of the century?

505) In the 1954 Cotton Bowl, Tommy Lewis made history by tackling Dicky Moegle on the 38 yard line. Why?

506) What history making event did Ben Abruzzo, Max Anderson and Larry Newman complete in 1978?

507) Who pitched 12 innings of *perfect* ball and still lost?

508) Olga Korbat won how many gold medals in the 1976 Montreal Olympics?

509) Who was the first driver to win two Daytona 500's?

510) Who was the tallest fighter to win the heavyweight title?

. . . Answers

500. Clint Hartung & Whitey Lockman

501. The only women to win the "Grand Slam of Tennis"

502. Lee Elder in 1974

503. Pitcher Joe Nuxhall, 15 yrs., 10 mos.

504. George Mikan

505. He sprang off his team bench to do it.

506. First trans-Atlantic balloon crossing.

507. Harvey Haddox lost 1-0 in 13 innings against the Braves, 6/26/59

508. None

509. Richard Petty

510. Primo Carnera

511) What percentage (within 5%) of a runner's energy is expended in overcoming air resistance in a 100 meter sprint?

512) What number did St. Louis Brown's midget Eddie Gaedel wear?

513) Jessie Owens was fast, but did he ever outrun a racehorse?

514) Who was the first golfer to win over $100,000 in a year?

515) Four Notre Dame quarterbacks have won Heisman Trophies. How many can you name?

516) What is "Teddy Ballgame"?

517) Who was the first heavyweight champ under the Marquis of Queensbury Rules?

518) Who is the only Olympic runner to win the 100 meter dash twice?

519) What is the circumference of a basketball?

520) How many teams have won more than one Superbowl?

521) What is the record for most consecutive games to hit safely?

. . . Answers

511. 20%

512. His uniform number was 1/8

513. Yes, 1936 in a 100 yard race

514. Arnold Palmer

515. Angelo Bertelli, Johnny Lujack, Paul Hornung and John Huarte

516. One of Ted Williams favorite nicknames.

517. James J. Corbett

518. Wyomia Tyus

519. 30 inches

520. 4 — Dallas, Green Bay, Pittsburgh & Miami

521. 56 — Joe DiMaggio

QUESTIONS

522) Who was the first American woman gymnist to win a medal in international competition?

523) What feat did Bob Beamon perform in the 1968 Olympics?

524) What three different color flags are used to mark the course in Alpine downhill skiing?

525) What major league team was involved in all three; the longest game in terms of time, the longest in terms of innings and the longest scoreless game?

526) What rule change was made in 1937 which sped up the game of basketball significantly?

527) Entertainer Tiny Tim is an avid fan of what sport?

528) Who was known as the "Clown Prince of Baseball"?

529) If the line of scrimmage is the 17 yard line, how far would the football have to travel for a field goal?

530) In golf, what does having "the honor" entitle a player to?

Identify the famous football player by his team and jersey number:

531) 00 on Oakland

532) 5 on Green Bay

. . . Answers

522. Cathy Rigby

523. Longest long-jump ever, 29 feet, 2½ inches

524. Red, yellow and blue

525. N.Y. Mets; 7 hrs. 32 min., 25 innings & 24 innings

526. Eliminated the center jump after each field goal

527. Hockey

528. Al Schacht

529. 34 yards — seven yards for the snap and the goal posts are set back 10 yards.

530. Tee off first

531. Jim Otto

532. Paul Hornung

QUESTIONS

Identify the famous football player by his team and jersey number:

533) 10 on Minnesota

534) 12 on N.Y. Jets

535) 14 on N.Y. Giants

536) 19 on Baltimore

537) 32 on Cleveland

538) 40 on Chicago

539) 42 on N.Y. Giants

540) 77 on Chicago

541) If a kid hits a spaulding 3 sewers, what game is he playing?

542) How many members on a track relay team?

543) A Brooklyn and a Jersey are found in what game?

544) What is the name of the technique used by novice skiers to slow down or stop?

545) When Bob Watson scored from 2nd base on a three run home run by Milt May on May 4, 1975, what baseball milestone was achieved?

. . . Answers

533. Fran Tarkenton

534. Joe Namath

535. Y.A. Tittle

536. Johnny Unitas

537. Jim Brown

538. Gale Sayers

539. Charlie Connerly

540. Red Grange

541. Stickball, a city street game.

542. Four

543. Bowling

544. Snow Plow

545. Scored the major leagues 1,000,000th run

546) If Chris Economaki is announcing the event on television, you're probably watching what sport?

547) What is the diameter of a basketball hoop?

548) How long is half-time in pro football?

549) The world record for the 440 relay was established by a team from UCLA. One of its members went on to become an NFL great. Name him.

550) In ten pin bowling, how many pins are set up across the back row.

551) Two brothers playing for the same team hit home runs in the same game on three separate occasions. Name them.

552) What do the following dates have in common? Sept. 18, 1897, Sept. 11, 1904, July 28, 1905, July 7, 1906, July 18, 1908 and Aug. 27, 1908.

553) The Portsmouth Spartans became what NFL team?

554) Do you know what the record is for most consecutive gutter balls?

555) Football's great receiver Kyle Rote has a son who is a sports great himself. In what sport?

. . . Answers

546. Auto racing

547. 18 inches

548. 15 minutes

549. O.J. Simpson

550. Four—7,8,9,10

551. Hank Aaron and Tommie Aaron

552. They're all listed as Satchel Paige's birthdate.

553. Detroit Lions

554. 19 by Rich Caplette, Danielson, Ct., Sept. 7, 1971

555. Kyle Rote Jr., plays pro-soccer

556) What unique event took place between Stan Musial of the Cards and Chicago's Frankie Baumholtz in the last game of the 1952 season?

557) Who won the NBA's first 3 point scoring title?

558) Who was the first Little League player to go on to play in the majors? (hint, he pitched for Milwaukee Braves)

559) Where did Earl Monroe play his college ball?

560) In what sport is a "Reuther board" used?

561) A "training cart" is used in what sport?

562) What major rearrangement took place in the NHL in 1974?

563) This ex-major league umpire went on to call the plays for NBC's Game of the Week. Name him.

564) Miami defeated Kansas City 27–24 in the AFC playoff in 1971. What distinction does this game hold.

565) Ted St. Martin says he's the best at what he does and travels around the country making a living at it. What is it?

566) Monty Hall "Let's Make a Deal" is a fan of, and used to be an announcer for what sport?

. . . Answers

556. Musial pitched and lefty Baumholtz batted righty

557. Fred Brown—Seattle Supersonics

558. Joey Jay

559. Francis Marion College

560. Gymnastics

561. Harness racing

562. Two conferences are formed, Wales & Campbell

563. Ron Luciano

564. Longest in NFL History

565. Top basketball free throw shooter. Holds the record with 2,036 in a row.

566. Hockey

567) What does $1,885.50 represent.

568) What is Sue Sedlacek famous for?

569) E. J. Holub played in Super Bowl I and Super Bowl IV with the Kansas City Chiefs. What special distinction did he earn?

Match these famous sports stars with their nickname.

570) The Horse	a. Leo Durocher
571) Charlie Hustle	b. Pete Rose
572) Golden Boy	c. Paul Hornung
573) Hammerin' Hank	d. Alan Ameche
574) The Count	e. Ed Jones
575) The Lip	f. Stan Musial
576) The Man	g. John Havlicek
577) Crazy Legs	h. Billy Johnson
578) The Iron Horse	i. Ron Guidry
579) Louisiana Lightning	j. Hank Aaron
580) Dandy	k. Richard Lane
581) Night Train	l. Lou Gehrig
582) The Toe	m. Elroy Hirsch
583) Too Tall	n. Lou Groza
584) White Shoes	o. John Montefusco
585) Hondo	p. Jack Nicklaus
586) Golden Bear	q. Don Merideth

. . . Answers

567. The record payout for a $2.00 horse bet.

568. Most successful female horse trainer.

569. He played defense in I and offense in IV. Only player ever to do so.

570. d.
571. b.
572. c.
573. j.
574. o.
575. a.
576. f.
577. m.
578. l.
579. i.
580. q.
581. k.
582. n.
583. e.
584. h.
585. g.
586. p.

587) When Joe Foss resigned as commissioner of the AFL in 1966, who replaced him?

588) Which press associations select the number one college team in the nation?

589) As a young man, this future former U.S. president could out wrestle any man in his home county in Illinois.

590) What are the four Olympic throwing events?

591) How many NHL teams are Canadian?

592) Who has the most career homeruns, Joe DiMaggio or Ted Williams?

593) Where did the N.Y. Giants play their last five games of 1973?

594) Who is the Podoloff trophy awarded to?

. . . *Answers*

587. Al Davis

588. Associated Press & United Press International

589. Abe Lincoln

590. Javelin, discus, shotput & hammer

591. 7

592. Ted Williams — 521 vs. 361

593. Yale Bowl

594. MVP of NBA

595) What astounding feat did 16-year old Robin Lee Graham perform in 1970?

596) What is a full count?

597) *Chariots of Fire* portrays the events of which Olympics?

598) Until 1972, Ring Belts were awarded to champions by . . . ?

599) How many teams are in the NHL?

600) The "Miracle Mets" of 1969 won the World Series. In what other year did they play in the World Series?

601) When the NFL expanded in 1960, what new team was added?

602) Who was the first commissioner of the ABA?

603) The first night baseball game was played between which two teams?

. . . *Answers*

595. Sailed around the world alone.

596. 3 balls and 2 strikes

597. 1924, Paris

598. Ring Magazine

599. 21

600. 1973, Oakland beat them in 7 games.

601. Dallas

602. George Mikan

603. Cincinnati & Philadelphia

604) Who was the youngest decathlon gold medal champion?

605) Brothers Joe and Vince Dundee hold what distinction?

606) The Atlanta Braves used to reside in which other two cities?

607) Who were the only two NHL players to win the MVP for Stanley Cup play more than once?

608) An "aspirin tablet" is a slang description for what?

609) In 1966, which franchise became the NFL's 15th team?

610) What major sports shrine is located in Springfield, Mass.?

611) What kind of play might be described as 6-4-3?

612) Who owns the most Olympic speed skating medals?

613) What is the penalty for "icing the puck" in a hockey game?

614) Bab Dedrikson married George Zaharias who was a champion in what professional sport?

615) Two pitchers share 2nd place in career wins with 373. Name them.

... *Answers*

604. Bob Mathias, 17 years old.

605. Both were World Boxing Champions

606. Boston & Milwaukee

607. Bobby Orr & Bernie Parent

608. Nolan Ryan's fastball

609. Atlanta Falcons

610. Naismith Mem. Basketball Hall of Fame

611. Double play

612. Lydia Skoblikova, USSR 1960—64; 6 total

613. Face-off in offending team's defensive zone.

614. Wrestling

615. Grover Cleveland Alexander & Christy Mathewson

616) In what sport do you find a massé shot?
    a. Tennis   c. Golf
    b. Billiards   d. Archery

617) How much time is a basketball player allowed to make a "throw in"?
    a. 5 sec.   c. 15 sec.
    b. 10 sec.   d. 20 sec.

618) Olympic speed skating is run at how many distances?
    a. 3   c. 5
    b. 4   d. 6

619) Who is the only pitcher to hit a grand slam home run in a World Series game?
    a. Darold Knowles   c. Dave McNally
    b. Jim Bunning   d. Nolan Ryan

620) The record for non-stop long distance swimming is . . . ?
    a. 37 miles   c. 166 miles
    b. 84 miles   d. 292 miles

621) A "trudgen stroke" is used in what sport?
    a. Tennis   c. Swimming
    b. Golf   d. Billiards

. . . Answers

616. b. billiards

617. a. 5 sec.

618. c. 5

619. c. Dave McNally (game 3 of the 1970 series)

620. d. 292 miles (St. Louis to the mouth of the Mississippi)

621. c. swimming

622) The Brooklyn Dodgers played 15 home games over two seasons ('56 & '57) outside of Ebbets Field. Where?
   a. Polo Grounds, Manhattan
   b. Yankee Stadium, Bronx
   c. Roosevelt Stadium, Jersey City
   d. Randalls Island Stadium

623) What is the lowest season output in stolen bases to ever lead the American League? By whom?
   a. 15   c. 37
   b. 28   d. 41

624) What is the name of the N.Y. sports writer who persuaded Madison Square Garden to put on the first college basketball double header in 1934?
   a. Bill Mulligan   c. Bill Stern
   b. Ned Irish   d. Howard Garfinkel

625) In figure skating, what is the name given to a toe loop performed counter clockwise?
   a. Lutz   c. Salchow
   b. Inside loop   d. Axel

626) What do you call the colored lights that control the start of a drag race?

627) Name the US athlete who won the Olympic gold medal 4 times in the Discus Throw?

628) In what game is a player sometimes brushed back?

. . . Answers

622. c. Roosevelt Stadium, Jersey City (7 in 1956, 8 in 1957)

623. a. 15 (Dom DiMaggio in 1950)

624. b. Ned Irish

625. a. Lutz

626. Christmas tree

627. Al Oerter

628. Baseball

629) In 1966 which was the first expansion team in history to win a division or conference title?

630) Who was the last American League MVP to be a switch hitter?

631) This future movie actor won 5 gold medals in the 1924 and 1928 Olympics for swimming. Name him.

632) Ken Norton held the heavyweight crown in a boxing association. WBA or WBC.

633) Which NHL star played for four decades?

634) Who has the most career wins for a pitcher with 511?

635) Who is the 5 time winner of off-road racing's "Mint 500" at Las Vegas?

636) What is the only movie made about a professional golfer?

637) What would Tracy Stallard rather not be remembered for?

638) Who did Bud Grant replace as head coach of the Minnesota Vikings in 1967?

639) An NBA game is divided into four periods. How long is each one?

. . . Answers

629. Dallas

630. Vida Blue (whenever he bats, it is from either side of the plate)

631. Johnny Weissmuller

632. WBC

633. Gordie Howe

634. Cy Young

635. Walker Evans

636. "Follow the Sun", Glenn Ford played Ben Hogan

637. Pitcher Roger Maris' 61st homerun

638. Van Brocklin

639. 12 minutes

640) This swimmer went on to a movie career after winning the gold medal at the 1932 Olympics. Name him.

641) Who was the originator of Ring Magazine?

642) Originally eliminated during World War II to save energy, the NHL just recently reinstated it. What is it?

643) What ex-major league ball park had the reputation for having both longest and shortest homerun territory?

644) He won auto racing's NASCAR Grand National Championship 4 out of 5 years between 1971–1975. Name him.

645) What do these names all have in common, Joe Platak, Jim Jacobs and Al Banuet?

646) Who was the first skier to win all three Alpine events in one Olympiad?

647) In 1968, who returned to pro-football as part owner and head coach of the expansion team, Cincinnati Bengals?

648) A college basketball game is divided in what manner?

649) What team did the US ice hockey team defeat for the gold medal in the 1980 Olympics?

. . . Answers

640. Buster Crabbe

641. Nat Fleisher

642. Overtime period

643. Polo Grounds—center & right field

644. Richard Petty

645. They are handball players

646. Austria's Anton Sailer in 1956

647. Paul Brown

648. Two 20 minute halves

649. Finland

650) Wilt Chamberlain played professionally for three years with what team before beginning his NBA career.

651) On November 8, 1970, who kicked a 63 yard field goal for the New Orleans Saints against the Detroit Lions?

652) Who was named MVP in the Mets Miracle World Series in 1969?

653) In World Track & Field, track events are always run counter clockwise. True or False?

654) When a referee feels a fighter is unable to defend himself, the fight may be stopped and a TKO awarded. The winning fighter gets credit for a "knock-out". True or False?

655) In 1979 when the Pirates won the World Series, Willie Stargell was MVP and led the league in strike-outs as well. True or False?

656) In a PGA sanctioned match, the penalty for a player forgetting to sign the score card is tournament elimination. True or False?

657) Despite his great career with L.A. Lakers, Jerry West has never won the NBA Scoring Championship. True or False?

658) Monty Stratton, after losing a leg in a gunshot ac-cident, returned to pitch again in the majors. True or False?

. . . *Answers*

650. Harlem Globe Trotters

651. Tom Dempsey

652. Don Clendenon

653. True

654. True

655. True

656. True

657. False

658. False (but he did pitch in the minors)

659) Man O' War was upset by an 8-1 choice by the name of Upset. True or False?

660) In 1950, top ranked Bradley lost both the NIT & NCAA tournaments to CCNY. True or False?

661) No Ivy League team has ever won the Rose Bowl. True or False?

662) There is no difference between a Trotter and a Pacer in Harness Racing. True or False?

663) In the 1905 Kentucky Derby, Layson finished both third and dead last. True or False?

664) J. Paul Getty at one time was Jack Dempsey's sparring partner. True or False?

665) Along with all her other major accomplishments, Babe Dedrikson also won 2 gold and 1 silver medal in the 1932 Olympics. True or False?

666) In 1931 Clessie Cummins completed the INDY 500 without a single pit stop. True or False?

667) Jackie Robinson played for the Dodgers in both Brooklyn and Los Angeles. True or False?

668) When Weeb Ewbank retired as head coach of the Jets he was replaced by his son-in-law. True or False?

. . . *Answers*

659. True (his only defeat)

660. True

661. False (Columbia did in 1934)

662. False

663. True (it was a 3 horse race)

664. True

665. True

666. True (it was a diesel)

667. False

668. True (Charlie Winner)

669) Which player of the Minnesota Vikings completed a string in which he made at least one field goal in 31 consecutive games between 1968 and 1970?

670) Ewa Klobukowska, an Olympic sprinter, holds what dubious distinction?

671) What is the difference between a perfect baseball game and a no-hitter?

672) Who became the head coach of the Washington Redskins in 1969?

673) Who was the team leader and voted MVP when the Knicks won their only NBA championship?

674) The original Washington Senators are now which team?

675) In 1975, who was the last of the original Raiders to retire after 15 years as one of the great centers in football history?

676) Who won the light welterweight gold medal in the 1976 Olympics?

677) How many times has the American League won the All-Star game between 1970 & 1980?

678) Who replaced Allie Sherman in 1969 when he was fired as head coach of the New York Giants?

. . . Answers

669. Fred Turner

670. She was the first female athlete to fail the sex test.

671. Perfect game 27 up & 27 down. No hitter may have base runners from walks, errors, etc.

672. Vince Lombardi

673. Willis Reed

674. Minnesota Twins

675. Jim Otto

676. Ray Leonard

677. Only once — 1971

678. Alex Webster

679) What university has developed the most NBA players?

680) Who are the famous pitching brothers, Phil & Joe?

681) In 1971, which player of the Minnesota Vikings was named the NFC MVP and he was the first lineman ever to receive the honor.

682) Which two super heavyweight gold medalists went on to become heavyweight champions of the world?

683) Reggie Jackson holds many records, one of which he would probably be willing to forget, what is it?

684) Which 1968 Heisman trophy winner was the number one draft pick of the Buffalo Bills in 1969?

685) What selection process brought Bob Cousy to the Celtics?

686) The Royals hail from Kansas City, Kansas or Kansas City, Missouri?

687) In the 1974 AFC championship game, Pittsburgh's defense held which team to a record-low 29 yards rushing?

688) Who won the middleweight gold medal in the 1952 Olympics?

. . . Answers

679. UCLA

680. Niekro

681. Alan Page

682. Joe Frazier & George Foreman

683. Strike-out king

684. O.J. Simpson

635. Picked from a hat.

686. Missouri

687. Oakland

688. Floyd Patterson

689) Ronald Reagan used to broadcast Cubs baseball for a radio station in what city?

690) Before adopting the 9 inning limit, how was a baseball game decided?

691) In 1969, who became the new head coach of the Oakland Raiders?

692) How many players are on the ice for a penalty shot in hockey?

693) What is the college record for the longest basketball field goal?

694) Where was the first All-Star baseball game played?

695) Patricia McCormick made her professional debut on Jan. 20, 1952 in what sports attraction?

696) This female track star suffered through polio, double pneumonia and scarlet fever as a child, yet won 3 gold medals in the 1960 Olympics. Name her.

697) Hank Bauer, Yogi Berra and Joe Pepitone admitted publicly that they were sissies. What was the circumstance?

698) The first official World Series was played in 1905. Who represented each league?

Answers

689. Des Moines, Iowa

690. First team to score 21 runs

691. John Madden

692. 1 skater and 1 goalie

693. 89 feet, 3 inches

694. Comiskey Park, Chicago

695. Bull fighting

696. Wilma Rudolf

697. Ozon Hairspray commercial

698. The N.Y. Giants (NL) beat the Philadelphia Athletics (AL)

699) In 1961, Baltimore's first draft choice was a running back from Ohio State. What was his name?

700) When famous announcer Clem McCarthy would call a horse race, how did he keep track of the field:
    a. Jockey's riding position
    b. Color of jockey's silks
    c. Color of the horse
    d. Number on saddle

701) The lowest season output for a major league homerun title was . . . ?
    a. 6
    b. 13
    c. 19
    d. 27

702) The diameter of a tennis ball is . . . ?
    a. 2.0 inches
    b. 2.5 inches
    c. 3.0 inches
    d. 3.5 inches

703) In gymnastics, a rapid straightening from a pike position is called . . . ?
    a. a pike
    b. a salto
    c. a kip
    d. a vault

. . . Answers

699. Tom Matte

700. b. Color of jockey's silks

701. a. 6

702. b. 2.5 inches

703. c. a kip

704) The odds against a golfer making a hole in one are . . . ?

    a. 300 to 1

    b. 3,000 to 1

    c. 300,000 to 1

    d. 3,000,000 to 1

705) The first Heisman Trophy was awarded in 1935. Who won it?

    a. Red Grange

    b. Jay Berwanger

    c. Charlie Connerly

    d. None of the above

706) The Lady Byng Trophy is awarded to the NHL player who is chosen for . . . ?

    a. Outstanding rookie

    b. Excels defensively

    c. Gentlemanly conduct

    d. MVP in Stanley Cup game

707) The St. Andrews Golfing Club in Yonkers, N.Y. (oldest continuing club in U.S.) was originally how long?

    a. 6 holes

    b. 9 holes

    c. 15 holes

    d. 22 holes

708) Second and long is a term used in which sport?

    a. Baseball   c. Hockey

    b. Football   d. Rodeo

. . . *Answers*

704. c. 300,000 to 1

705. b. Jay Berwanger

706. c. Gentlemanly conduct

707. a. 6 holes

708. b. Football

09) Earl Morrall led the Baltimore Colts to the Super Bowl after being traded from which team?

    a. Detroit Lions

    b. N.Y. Giants

    c. Cleveland Browns

    d. Pittsburgh Steelers

10) The Miami Dolphins had their 18 game winning streak ended when they lost to . . .

    a. N.Y. Jets

    b. Dallas Cowboys

    c. L.A. Rams

    d. Oakland Raiders

11) Bill Bradley played his college ball at . . . ?

    a. Rutgers

    b. William and Mary

    c. Princeton

    d. Notre Dame

12) Who was Joe Louis referring to when he said, "He an run, but he can't hide"?

    a. Billy Conn

    b. Max Schmeling

    c. Jersey Joe Walcott

    d. Buddy Baer

13) How many people were on hand in Mudville when Mighty Casey" struck out?

    a. 500   c. 5000

    b. 1000   d. 10,000

. . . Answers

709. b. N.Y. Giants

710. d. Oakland Raiders

711. c. Princeton

712. a. Billy Conn

713. c. 5,000 ("10,000 eyes were on him")

714) The width in yards of a football field?
  a. 40 5/6
  b. 53 1/3
  c. 60
  d. 70 1/4

715) The 1911–191? Philadelphia Athletics had which of the following titles associated with it?
  a. The Whiz Kids
  b. Murderer's Row
  c. Gashouse Gang
  d. $100,000 Infield

716) What NHL defenseman won the James Norris Trophy a record 8 times?

717) What is the highest season batting average to win the batting title? Who owns it?

718) What did the CCNY basketball team achieve in 1950?

719) What major league baseball field does not have lights?

720) What famous entertainer fought under the name Packey East?

721) Mohammad Ali won his Olympic gold medal in 1960 in what weight class?

. . . Answers

714. b. 53⅓

715. d. $100,000 infield

716. Bobby Orr — 8 years running

717. .424 by Roger Hornsby in 1924

718. Only team to ever win the NCAA & NIT championship in one year.

719. Wrigley Field

720. Bob Hope

721. Light Heavyweight

722) Who won the first American League-National League All Star game ever played?

723) Who was the cornerback from Michigan State who was Green Bay's first draft choice in 1961?

724) What NHL team has won the Stanley Cup most times since 1950?

725) Who holds the record for career stolen bases? How many?

726) What is James Naismith credited for?

727) Who was the starting 2nd baseman of the original N.Y. Mets?

728) What pitcher had a career record of 29–48, but had Babe Ruth's number, striking him out 10 times in a row and 19 out of 31 at bats.

729) What was unique about Hanni Wenzel winning the slalom and giant slalom gold medal in the 1980 Olympics?

730) In what city was the first major league night baseball game played?

731) Who was the quarterback from N.C. State who was the number one draft pick of the Oakland Raiders in 1962?

. . . Answers

722. American League (4-2)

723. Herb Adderly

724. Montreal Canadians, 16 times—1950-1983

725. Lou Brock, 938

726. Inventing the game of basketball

727. Charlie Neil

728. Hubert Pruett—St. Louis Browns

729. 1st ever from the tiny nation of Lichtenstein

730. Cincinnati

731. Roman Gabriel

732) What is the least number of skaters a team can skate with, not counting the goalie.

733) What is Casey Stengel's full name?

734) Who holds the NHL record for most points in a game?

735) John Havlicek retired from basketball having scored 1000 or more points for a record number of seasons. How many?

736) What letter on a score card represents a strike out?

737) Who was the first NHL player to earn a $100,000 a year salary?

738) Gymnast Larissa Latynina holds what Olympic distinction?

739) In 1963, the Los Angeles Rams had a massive defensive line called the "Fearsome Foursome" including Deacon Jones, Rosey Grier and Merlin Olsen. Who was the fourth member?

740) What nickname was given to Detroit pitcher Mark Fidrych?

741) For what accomplishment is the Art Ross Trophy awarded in the NHL?

. . . Answers

732. 3 skaters

733. Charles Dillon Stengel

734. Darryl Sittler with 10

735. 16

736. K

737. Bobby Orr

738. Most medals of any athlete with 18, 9 gold, 5 silver & 4 bronze

739. Lamar Lundy

740. "The Bird"

741. Highest number scoring points in a season.

742) What year was the first NCAA college basketball championship played?

743) Oakland is the A's third home city. Name the other two.

744) NBA star George Mikan had a brother who also played NBA ball. Name his brother.

745) Who set a new pro record when he ran for 243 yards against the Jets on December 8, 1963?

746) Heisman Trophy winner George Rogers signed to play with the New Orleans Jazz. True or False?

747) It's a fact that some martial-arts masters can dodge a bullet. True or False?

748) Frank Robinson is the only player to win MVP in both leagues. True or False?

749) Slugger Frank "Home Run" Baker never hit more than 12 home runs in a season. True or False?

750) In tennis, a soft, high shot is called a volley. True or False?

751) No basketball player has ever made it to the pros directly from high school. True or False?

752) When Roger Maris hit 61 home runs, none of them were grands slams. True or False?

. . . *Answers*

742. 1939

743. Kansas City & Philadelphia

744. Ed

745. Cookie Gilchrist

746. False (New Orleans Saints)

747. False

748. True

749. True

750. False (It's called a lob)

751. False (Moses Malone did it)

752. True

753) Bill Russell was never selected as the NBA Rookie of the Year. True or False?

754) A player may advance the ball in soccer by dribbling. True or False?

755) A skier is allowed only one trial run before skiing the slalom. True or False?

756) Doc Blanchard and Glenn Davis both won the Heisman Trophy in successive years. True or False?

757) The St. Louis Browns had a midget on their team once. His job was to pinch hit and draw a base on balls. True or False?

758) Who was the first heavyweight champion to retire while holding the title?

759) Where did Jackie Robinson play organized baseball before joining the Brooklyn Dodgers?

760) Marguerite Norris Riker is the only woman to have her name inscribed on the Stanley Cup. What was the circumstance?

761) Which San Francisco 49er completed a string in which he kicked 234 consecutive extra points between 1959 & 1965?

762) What are the longest and shortest outfield fences in the major leagues today?

. . . *Answers*

753. True (Maurice Stokes beat him out)

754. True (Yep, in soccer too!)

755. False (No trial runs are allowed.)

756. True (1945, 1946)

757. True (43 inch Eddie Gaedel)

758. Jim Jeffries — 1905

759. Montreal Royals

760. She owned the 1952 cup winning Detroit Red Wings

761. Tommy Davis

762. Metropolitan Stadium, Minn., 430′ center field and Yankee Stadium, N.Y., 313′ right field.

763) Where was the first NCAA college basketball championship game played?

764) Before becoming the Baltimore Orioles, they were known as . . . ?

765) Jim Arender was the first American to win a first place in what international competition?

766) Rookie of the Year honors were first awarded in the NL & AL in what years?

767) Who was high scorer for the Knicks in the game when Wilt Chamberlain scored 100 points against them?

768) In 1965, what was the name of the playoff bowl played between the runner-ups in each division of the NFL?

769) What was the original name of the Houston Astros?

770) What was the first overtime football game in the NFL?

771) Who was the oldest player to get a hit in a major league ball game?

772) What major innovation to bowling was introduced in 1952?

. . . *Answers*

763. Northwestern University, Oregon

764. St. Louis Browns

765. Sky Diving — 1960

766. NL — 1947 and AL — 1948.

767. Richie Guerin

768. Bert Bell Benefit Bowl

769. Colt 45's

770. The 1958 Colts-Giants championship game

771. Minnie Minoso, 53 years, 9 months

772. Automatic pin setter

773) In 1926 he had a record of 23–12 and led the league with a 1.75 ERA pitching for the Boston Red Sox. Name him.

774) An entire team once had the same batting averages after a game as before it. How come?

775) Who were the first two Americans to win Olympic medals in Men's Alpine Skiing?

776) Who owns the record for most career hits?

777) While we're at it, did Ty Cobb bat righty or lefty?

778) How many teams are there in the NBA?

779) Since its inception in 1933, the All-Star Game has been played every year except?

780) In what year did the U.S. men's gymnastic team win its first ever medal in world competition?

781) Bob Gibson and Nolan Ryan both threw their 3000th strike out past the same batter. Who owns this dubious distinction?

782) The Baltimore Colts/New York Giants championship game of 1958 was called the greatest game ever played. Who did the play-by-play?

783) Name the pitcher who has 4 no-hitters, including a perfect game, to his credit.

. . . Answers

773. Babe Ruth

774. Chicago White Sox were "no-hit" by Bob Feller on opening day of the season.

775. Billy Kidd & Jimmy Heuga placed 2nd & 3rd in 1964

776. Ty Cobb, 4,191 hits

777. Lefty

778. 22

779. 1945

780. 1979

781. Cesar Geronimo

782. Chuck Thompson of Baltimore

783. Sandy Koufax

784) Who was the first draft choice of Green Bay in 1957?

785) Who is the first woman golfer to earn over $100,000 in one season?

786) What team established "Ladies Day" at baseball games?

787) Its real name is the "International Lawn Tennis Challenge Trophy", but is better known as what?

788) Who is credited with developing the first "wet suit" used in swimming?

Match the husband and wife teams:

789) Joe DiMaggio   a. Joey Heatherton

790) Leo Durocher   b. Terry Moore

791) Bob Waterfield   c. Marilyn Monroe

792) Jack Dempsey   d. JoJo Starbuck

793) Glenn Davis   e. Jane Russell

794) Lance Rentzel   f. Estelle Taylor

795) Terry Bradshaw   g. Larraine Day

. . . Answers

784. Paul Hornung of Notre Dame

785. Judy Rankin

786. St. Louis Browns

787. The Davis Cup

788. Ben Franklin, honest!

789. c.

790. g.

791. e.

792. f.

793. b.

794. a.

795. d.

QUESTIONS

Identify the baseball star from his real name listed below.

796) Sanford Braun

797) Andrew Nordstrum

798) George Koslowski

799) Edmund Lopatyaski

800) Cornelius McGillicuddy

801) Alfred Pesano

802) John Peyeskovich

803) What was the number of the golf club used by astronaut Alan Shepard on the moon?

804) Which football teams played in the legendary Heidi Game in 1968?

805) Players from which college have won the most Heisman trophies?

806) What was the nickname of the 1906 Chicago White Sox baseball team?

807) Which sport has two Halls of Fame, one in Canada and one in the United States?

808) What is the nickname of Yankee Stadium?

. . . Answers

796. Sandy Koufax

797. Andy Carey

798. Dave Koslo

799. Eddie Lopat

800. Connie Mack

801. Billy Martin

802. Johnny Pesky

803. The 6 iron

804. N.Y. Jets and Oakland Raiders

805. Notre Dame

806. "The Hitless Wonders"

807. Hockey

808. The house that Ruth built.

809) What five Hall of Famers did Carl Hubbel strike out in succession during the 1934 All-Star game?

810) What do the winners of the INDY 500 traditionally drink in the winner's circle?

811) What nickname is given to both an automatic pitching machine and Jack Dempsey's right hand?

812) Name the eight colleges in the Ivy League Conference.

813) Where is the Jockey's Hall of Fame located?

814) Who is Charlie Brown's favorite baseball player?

815) Name the champion boxer in the comic strip created by Ham Fisher.

816) When is Lou Gehrig Day celebrated at Yankee Stadium?

817) What is the traditional day on which the Kentucky Derby is run?

818) Who was the first bowler to bowl a 300 game in an ABC Championship match?

819) The Lange Cup is awarded in what sport?

820) How many pitches did Don Larsen throw in his famous perfect game in the 1956 World Series?

. . . Answers

809. Babe Ruth, Lou Gehrig, Jimmy Foxx, Al Simmons & Joe Cronin

810. They drink milk

811. Iron Mike

812. Brown, Columbia, Cornell, Dartmouth, Harvard, Pennsylvania, Princeton & Yale

813. Detroit, Michigan

814. Joe Shlabotnik

815. Joe Palooka

816. July 4th

817. The first Sat. in May

818. William J. Knox

819. Professional skiing

820. 97

821) What's the name of the trophy given to the winning team of the Super Bowl?

822) On Sept. 22, 1927, Lou Gehrig broke Babe Ruth's record of 170 runs batted in. Which also happened that day?

823) What was Cassius Clay's nickname?

824) What was the name of the only race horse to defeat Man O' War?

825) Who played in the most games as a Yankee?

826) What was Rocky Marciano's real name?

827) What is the song that's played before the Preakness Stakes every year?

828) Name the Mascots of these Military Academies; Army, Navy and Air Force.

829) What did President Gerald Ford do at the Memphis Classic Golf Tournament on June 8, 1977?

830) What is the name of the trophy given to the winner of the annual Michigan-Notre Dame football game?

831) What is the name of the U.S. Naval Academy's football team?

. . . Answers

821. Lombardi Trophy

822. The famous "Long Count" bout between Jack Dempsey & Gene Tunny

823. The Louisville Lip

824. Upset

825. Mickey Mantle

826. Rocco Marchegiano

827. Maryland, my Maryland

828. Mule, Goat & Falcon

829. He shot a hole-in-one.

830. The Megaphone Trophy

831. The Midshipman

832) What was the collective term used to describe these 1927 Yankees; Babe Ruth, Lou Gehrig, Bob Meusel and Tony Lazzari?

Can you remember the World Series winning and losing teams for the years listed below?

833) 1969

834) 1970

835) 1971

836) 1972

837) 1973

838) 1974

839) 1975

840) 1976

841) 1977

842) 1978

843) 1979

844) 1980

845) What is the score of a forfeited baseball game?

. . . Answers

832. Murderer's Row

Winner	Loser
833. Mets (NL)	Baltimore (AL)
834. Baltimore (AL)	Cincinnati (NL)
835. Pittsburgh (NL)	Baltimore (AL)
836. Oakland (AL)	Cincinnati (NL)
837. Oakland (AL)	New York (NL)
838. Oakland (AL)	Los Angeles (NL)
839. Cincinnati (NL)	Boston (AL)
840. Cincinnati (NL)	New York (AL)
841. New York (AL)	Los Angeles (NL)
842. New York (AL)	Los Angeles (NL)
843. Pittsburgh (NL)	Baltimore (AL)
844. Baltimore (AL)	Cincinnati (NL)

845. 9-0

846) What three baseball players played in 4 decades. The 1930's to the 1960's?

847) What does the "OJ" in O. J. Simpson's name stand for?

848) Who is the only pitcher to pitch a perfect game in relief?

849) Who boxed three rounds with Archie Moore, pitched in a pre-season game at Yankee Stadium and drove in an actual auto race without being a professional athlete?

850) Name the famous baseball catcher who hosted such game shows as "He Said, She Said", "Sale of the Century" and "The Memory Game".

851) What is the name of Georgia Tech's football team?

852) In the now defunct American Basketball Association, what was so unusual about the basketball they used?

853) What was the first pro baseball team?

854) On a regulation British dart board, what is the number on the top?

855) Who played the title role in the 1950 movie "The Jackie Robinson Story"?

. . . *Answers*

846. Early Wynn, '39-'63, Ted Williams, '39-'60 and Mickey Vernon, '39-'60.

847. Orenthal James

848. Ernie Shore

849. George Plimpton

850. Joe Garagiola

851. The Rambling Wrecks

852. It was red, white and blue.

853. Cincinnati Red Stockings

854. 20

855. Jackie Robinson played himself

856) Name the Rodeo "big three."

857) Whose record did Whitey Ford break for consecutive scoreless innings pitched in a world series?

858) Weight lifting became a permanent Olympic event in what year?

859) What is a "scroogie"?

860) Who was the offensive coach of the New York Giants when he was named head coach of the Green Bay Packers in 1959?

861) On Jan. 20, 1968, 53,000 fans showed up for a college basketball game between which two teams?

862) One of the original stars of Roller Derby was nicknamed "The Flash". Name him.

863) In baseball what is known as a "tweener"?

864) Pete Rozelle was named the new football commissioner in 1960. Who did he replace?

865) Where did the largest crowd ever assemble to watch a college basketball game?

866) When Jim Thorpe won the pentathlon in the 1912 Olympics, another famous American finished fifth in the same competition. Name him.

. . . Answers

856. Cheyenne Frontier Days, Calgary Stampede & Pendleton Roundup.

857. Babe Ruths

858. 1920 VII Olympic Games

859. It's a baseball pitch — screwball

860. Vince Lombardi

861. UCLA — Houston

862. Billy Bogash

863. A ball hit between two outfielders

864. Bert Bell

865. Houston Astro-Dome

866. Gen. George S. Patton

67) Who was the first black umpire in major league baseball?

68) In 1959 who was named quarterback of the decade after playing for the Los Angeles Rams and the Philadelphia Eagles?

69) The first east-west college all star basketball game was held where?

70) What is the first recorded outdoor game played by women in the U.S.?

71) What does it mean to "lay one down"?

72) In 1960, where did the Titans play their home games?

73) What famous college basketball coach has a "15 Point Pyramid for Success"?

74) The Wilson Wingate Trophy is awarded in what sport?

Select the correct answer for each of the following endurance records (non-stop).

75) Surfing
   a. 0.2 miles
   b. 1.4 miles
   c. 2.6 miles
   d. 3.1 miles

. . . *Answers*

867. Emmett Ashford

868. Norm Van Brocklin

869. Madison Square Garden

870. Croquet, during the civil war years

871. In baseball it means to bunt

872. The old Polo Grounds

873. UCLA's John Wooden

874. Lacrosse

875. c. 2.6 miles

Select the correct answer for each of the following
ndurance records (non-stop).

76) Hang Gliding
   a. 9.6 miles
   b. 23.3 miles
   c. 74.4 miles
   d. 110.6 miles

77) Skate Boarding
   a. 63 city blocks
   b. 486 swimming pool loops
   c. 196.2 kilometers
   d. 217.3 miles

Match the ball number to its color.

78) 1   a. blue stripe

79) 2   b. purple solid

80) 3   c. yellow stripe

81) 4   d. red stripe

82) 5   e. orange stripe

83) 6   f. red solid

84) 7   g. yellow solid

85) 8   h. green solid

. . . Answers

876. d. 110.6 miles

877. d. 217.3 miles

878. g.

879. o.

880. f.

881. b.

882. i.

883. h.

884. k.

885. l.

Match the ball number to its color.

86) 9   i. orange solid

87) 10   j. purple stripe

88) 11   k. plum solid

89) 12   l. black solid

90) 13   m. green stripe

91) 14   n. plum stripe

92) 15   o. blue solid

93) What is the minimum amount of time a bareback bull rider must stay on his animal to qualify?

94) How many members are there on a water polo team?

95) What is printed on Willie Mays' California license plate?

96) What do the letters in SCUBA stand for?

97) What position does Snoopy play on Charlie Brown's baseball team?

98) How often is the Soccer World Cup played for?

. . . Answers

886. c.

887. a.

888. d.

889. j.

890. e.

891. m.

892. n.

893. 6 seconds

894. 7

895. SAYHEY

896. Self-Contained Underwater Breathing Appa
     ratus

897. Shortstop

898. Every 4 years

899) In what 1956 movie did Paul Newman play Rocky Graziano?

900) Name the sports manufacturer who used to manufacture baseballs for the American and National leagues until 1976.

901) Mark Spitz is one of two olympians to hold the record for most total gold medals in the Olympics. Name the other one.

902) What is the full name of the man who donated the Stanley Cup to the NHL.

903) Who scored the first Super Bowl touchdown?

904) What is the nickname of pro-golfer Lee Trevino?

905) Where is the Swimming Hall of Fame located?

906) How many members are on a Canadian football team?

907) What number represents the answer to these three questions; the height of the crossbar on a goal post in football, the number on the football jersey worn by B. D. in the comic strip Doonsbury and the number on the football jersey worn by Mary Tyler Moore in her TV show?

908) How long is an Olympic marathon?

. . . Answers

899. "Somebody Up There Likes Me"

900. Spaulding

901. Paavo Nurmi

902. Frederick Arthur

903. Max McGee

904. Super Mex

905. Fort Lauderdale, Florida

906. 12

907. 10

908. 26 miles, 385 yards

909) What route is the Olympic marathon fashioned after?

910) How many fences must a horse jump in the Grand National Steeplechase in England?

911) In a horserace, what is the distance of one furlong?

912) Who replaced Lou Gehrig after his 2,130 consecutive baseball games?

913) What is the trophy awarded for the sport of badminton?

914) Who was the first winner of the Cy Young award?

915) Who was the sportscaster who made the famous outburst "the Giants have won the pennant" after Bobby Thompson hit his famous homerun?

916) Who was voted the outstanding athlete for the first half of the twentieth century?

917) On what team were the famous double-play trio Tinker to Evers to Chance?

918) What three things does a player lead the major leagues in when he wins the Triple Crown?

919) What three races does a horse win when he wins the Triple Crown?

. . . Answers

909. The distance from Marathon to Athens, Greece

910. 30

911. 220 yards

912. Babe Dahlgren

913. The Thomas Cup

914. Don Newcombe, 1956

915. Russ Hodges

916. Jim Thorpe

917. Chicago Cubs

918. Highest batting average, most home runs & most runs batted in.

919. Kentucky Derby, Preakness Stakes and Belmont Stakes

920) Where is the Trotting Horse Hall of Fame?

921) In baseball, who was the "Ugly Duckling"?

922) What was the first football team to use uniform numbers?

923) What is the only school in the world named for a baseball player?

The following actors had distinguished sport careers. Can you match them?

924) Kirk Douglas   a. Football—USC

925) Chuck Connors b. Dartmouth Heavyweight Boxing Champ

926) Alex Karas   c. Pro baseball—Dodgers

927) Alan Ladd   d. Football—Florida State

928) John Wayne   e. Swimming & diving—All American

929) Mike Connors   f. NFL—Detroit

930) Burt Reynolds g. Wrestling Champ.—St. Lawrence U.

931) Robert Ryan   h. Basketball—UCLA

. . . Answers

920. Goshen, N.Y.

921. Yogi Berra

922. University of Pittsburgh

923. Walter Johnson High School in Bethesda, Maryland

924. g.

925. c.

926. f.

927. e.

928. a.

929. h.

930. d.

931. b.

932) Which professional boxer weighs more, a feather-weight or a bantamweight?

933) Who was the first swimmer to break 1 minute in the 100 meters?

934) In the Abbott and Costello routine "who's on first", name the players of these certain positions: 1st base, 2nd base, 3rd base, shortstop, catcher, pitcher, left field, center field and right field.

935) How many divisionstle pl were there in the now defunct World Football League?

936) Who were the first champions in the now defunct World Tennis Association?

937) Jackie Jensen and Charles Essigian are the only two men to have done what?

938) What sports announcer gave Joe DiMaggio the nickname "Yankee Clipper"?

939) In Yankee Stadium what three players have memorial plaques devoted to them in center field.

940) The Boston Marathon is run on the same day each year. What day is it?

941) Chicago once hosted two NFL teams. The Bears are still there. Name the other team.

. . . Answers

932. Featherweight

933. Johnny Weissmuller

934. 1st base — Who
2nd base — What
3rd base — I don't know
shortstop — I don't care
catcher — Today
pitcher — Tomorrow
left field — Why
center field — Because
right field — they didn't have one

935. Three; Western, Central & Eastern

936. Denver Rackets in 1974

937. To play in the World Series & Rose Bowl

938. Arch McDonald

939. Miller Huggins, Lou Gehrig & Babe Ruth

940. April 19 — Patriot's Day

941. Cardinals — (they moved to St. Louis)

942) The N.Y. Knicks got bombed by a player who scored 100 points against them in a single game on March 2, 1962. Who dunnit?

943) In the Hollywood movie "Babe Comes Home" who played the role of "Babe Ruth"?

944) Who won the first American Football league crown in 1980?

945) What team did Y.A. Tittle play for before being traded to the Giants?

946) Who was the first American woman to win the world title in ice skating?

947) "Player of the Year" is the autobiography of what famous NFL player?

948) What is the record for most minutes played in a single college basketball game? It was set by Larry Costello when he played for Niagara.

949) The year Babe Ruth hit 60 homeruns he did not win MVP in the American League. Why?

950) Walter "Toots" Wright, Byron "Fats" Long, Willie "Kid" Oliver, Andy Washington and Al "Runt" Pullins all played on what team?

. . . Answers

942. Wilt Chamberlain

943. He played himself

944. Houston

945. 49'ers

946. Tenley Albright

947. Roman Gabriel

948. 70 minutes

949. There was a rule at the time that a player could not be a repeat winner. Ruth had won it the previous year.

950. The original Harlem Globetrotters

951) Who is the only basketball player to be named All-American in every year he was eligible in high school and college?

952) In the 1968 movie "Number One" who played the role of the New Orleans Saints' quarterback?

953) Three NFL teams do not represent a specific city or state. Name them.

954) Who was the fist man to pole vault 16 feet?

955) In Gale Sayers' autobiography "I'm Third", who is first?

956) How did Red Auerback indicate his team had the game "In the bag"?

957) In 1957, the National League's MVP and Cy Young Award winners were team mates. Name them.

958) Carol Polis is the first woman to be granted a license to judge what kind of sporting event?

959) Major league pitcher Bob Gibson also played some professional basketball. For what team?

. . . Answers

951. Jerry Lucas

952. Charleton Heston

953. Washington Redskins, D.C.
Football Giants
New England Patriots

954. John Uelses, Feb. 3, 1962

955. God

956. Lit his cigar

957. Hank Aaron & Warren Spahn, Milwaukee
Braves

958. Boxing

959. Harlem Globetrotters

Can you match the NBA season with its championship team? Note: There are repeat winners on list.

Season	Team
960) 1982–83	a. Los Angeles
961) 1981–82	b. Boston
962) 1980–81	c. Milwaukee
963) 1979–80	d. Portland
964) 1978–79	e. Seattle
965) 1977–78	f. New York
966) 1976–77	g. Washington
967) 1975–76	h. Golden State
968) 1974–75	i. Philadelphia
969) 1973–74	
970) 1972–73	
971) 1971–72	
972) 1970–71	

973) Who sponsored the first televised world series in 1947?

974) Who introduced the T-formation to football?

975) What do these NFL players have in common, Joe Guyan, Pete Calar & Jim Plunkett?

976) Where was the first bobsled run built in the U.S.?

977) According to a Boston Globe survey, the most knowledgeable sports fan as well as the most unruly are from what city?

. . . Answers

960. i.
961. a.
962. b.
963. a.
964. e.
965. g.
966. d.
967. b.
968. h.
969. b.
970. f.
971. a.
972. c.
973. Gillette Safety Razor Co. & Ford Motor Co.
974. George Halas — 1940 Chicago Bears
975. They are American Indians
976. Lake Placid for the 1932 Olympics
977. New York

978) Wilt Chamberlain, after leaving basketball, became the president of what association?

979) Whose home run won the 1960 World Series for Pittsburgh over the Yankees?

980) Who is the only man ever to win both the Pentathlon and Decathlon in the same Olympiad?

981) Who is the only NHL goalie to score a goal in an NHL game?

982) Who did Bart Starr replace as quarterback of the Green Bay Packers?

983) In the defunct WFL, the N.Y. Stars move on to become what franchise?

984) In what year was the first East-West College All-Star game held?

985) Who holds the record for most games played in a single baseball season?

986) Who holds the record for most strikeouts in a single game?

987) Who is the athlete credited with being the first to endorse commercial products.

988) Name the three events which make up harness racing's Triple Crown.

... Answers

978. President, International Volleyball Association

979. Bill Mazeroski

980. Jim Thorpe

981. Billy Smith, N.Y. Islanders, Nov. 28, 1979

982. Lamar McHan

983. Charlotte Hornets

984. March 30, 1946

985. Maury Wills — 165

986. Thomas Cheney, 21. (It was a 16 inning game)

987. Red Grange

988. Kentucky Futurity, Hambletonian & The Yonkers Trot.

QUESTIONS

989) Barney Oldfield was the first man to drive a mile a minute. What was the number on his famous Ford car?

990) Who was the first man to drive a car over 300 MPH? Hint: He did it on the Bonneville Salt Flats in Utah in 1935.

991) Who was the first non-American to win the Masters Golf Tournament?

992) Ken and Bob Forsch, as major league pitchers, hold what unique distinction?

993) Who was the coach of Georgia Tech when they defeated Cumberland by the score of 222–0?

994) Who was the first guard in pro basketball to score 1000 field goals in a season?

995) Who became the first NHL player to score a goal a game?

996) Over what distance is the Kentucky Derby run?

997) What record did Craig Breedlove set on Nov. 15, 1965?

998) In what sport are "silks" worn and by whom?

999) What type of skiing did Hans Gmoser pioneer in the Canadian Rockies?

1000) Founded the same year the Baseball Hall of Fame, it began with only 3 teams. It now boasts over 150,000 teams world wide. Name it.

1001) In what Ohio city did the Soap Box Derby originate?

. . . Answers

989. 999

990. Sir Malcolm Campbell, 301.13 MPH

991. Gary Player in 1961

992. They both pitched no hitters, Bob—1978, St. Louis Cards and Ken in 1979—Houston Astros.

993. John W. Heisman

994. Nate Archibald, '72-'73

995. Maurice Richard, 1944-45, 50 game season

996. A mile and a quarter

997. Land speech record in excess of 600 MPH (600.601)

998. Horse racing, by the Jockey

999. Helicopter Skiing

1000. Little League Baseball

1001. Dayton, Ohio